To Tom,
Enjoy,
Sharon
10-14-95

also by Sharon Loeschen

THE SECRETS OF SATIR
Collected Sayings of Virginia Satir

THE MAGIC OF SATIR

Practical Skills for Therapists

Virginia Satir

THE MAGIC OF SATIR

Practical Skills for Therapists

SHARON LOESCHEN, M.S.W., L.C.S.W.

Halcyon Publishing Design
Long Beach, California

1994

THE MAGIC OF SATIR
Practical Skills for Therapists

Frontispiece photograph of Virginia Satir by Jackie Schwartz

Library of Congress Catalog Card Number 91-75150
ISBN 0-9641340-0-4 *(previously ISBN 0-9627501-7-4)*

Printed in the United States of America

Third Printing, May, 1994

Published by Halcyon Publishing Design
4161 Hathaway Ave, Suite 45
Long Beach, California 90815

*To the furtherance
of the teachings
of Virginia Satir*

Preface

This book presents the philosophy and skills of Virginia Satir.

Because she believed deeply in the uniqueness of each human being and wanted her students to develop their own styles of therapy, Satir avoided teaching her skills directly. Her method of training was to model her approach to therapy, allowing others to take from it what they wished. She also provided students with intensive experiential workshops for personal growth. Satir was uniquely talented, very conscious of what she was doing, and not "shooting from the hip."

The opportunity for people to learn Satir's methods by watching her work or by experiencing her workshops was lost with her death. Because of this, I decided to write *The Magic of Satir.*

It is the premise of this work that much of what Satir did can be successfully learned and used by others. Included here are my conclusions on the tenents of her philosophy, the phases of her work, and the skills she used. You may be surprised to learn that her philosophy and many of her skills are applicable to working with individuals as well as couples and families.

My hope is that you will find inspiration from Virginia Satir's philosophy, and that this book will help you expand the repertory of your skills.

Sharon Loeschen

Long Beach, California
August 1991

Acknowledgments

I am most grateful to these people for their special contributions:

- Johanna Schwab, whose expertise and insights were invaluable;

- John Banmen, who added to my original conceptual framework and was one of my trainers for Module II of the Satir Training;

- Jane Gerber and Maria Gomori, who were my other trainers for Module II;

- Becky Thorn, who supported me and patiently read my many revisions;

- Pat Case, who was very enthusiastic about the work;

- Joan Howard, who encouraged me to add to my original text;

- Casey Perriman, who cheered me on, assuring me that the book would be of great value;

- Michelle Baldwin, Jim Bitter, and Anne Nerin, who were my trainers in Process Community VI of the Satir Training;

- Phil Reichline, who loaned me his tapes of Virginia Satir;

- John Baird, who gave me the idea for the title;

- Jackie Schwartz, who took the maginificent photograph of Virginia Satir that is the book's frontispiece;

- Susan Green LoNigro, for her work on the design of the book; and

- Sharon Olson, for her cheerful and professional work on the formatting and editing.

Contents

PHASE IV—PROMOTING ACCEPTANCE

PHASE V—MAKING CHANGES

PHASE VI—REINFORCING CHANGES

Practical Skills for Therapists

SATIR'S PHILOSOPHY

Satir's philosophy is the underpinning of all of her work and therefore of this work. Some of the tenets of her philosophy that the author derived from experiencing her teachings and her loving way of being with people are shared here to provide a basis for understanding her approach to therapy.

Enhancing self-worth is primary.

Satir used to say, "The job of a therapist is to help people have stars in their eyes—to truly feel their own value!"

Satir viewed people as manifestations of the life force, and therefore sacred. She believed people to be miracles and worthy of love. She described herself as looking beyond people's behavior and connecting with what she called their "pure spirit."

Satir saw people as having many inner resources that can be tapped in order to enhance their self-worth. These included the capacity to imagine, to create, to explore, to perceive accurately, to feel, to express, to choose, to be courageous, and to be wise.

She believed that these capacities or resources often become blocked, to a greater or lesser extent, by family and societal rules resulting in a lessened sense of self-worth.

For Satir, the level of a person's self-worth is the most important factor affecting behavior.

Nurturance is the way to bring about growth.

Satir believed that facilitating growth in humans is similar to that for plants, by creating a nourishing environment for them. Her philosophy was that symptomatic behaviors extinguish themselves naturally when strengths and inner resources are nurtured.

Satir saw a nourishing environment as one in which people experience being valued and are made to feel comfortable and safe. She once said, "You can't make a bean plant grow by jerking on it!"

Nurturance to Satir meant conveying respect and reverence for people as unique individuals. To her, uniqueness is a reflection of the miracle of life—that no two people on the face of the earth are exactly alike.

Nurturance to Satir also meant conveying to people that they are equal in personhood, no matter what their age, gender, race, position, or level of intelligence. She used to say, "All people have the same feelings whether they are two or ninety-two."

Awareness is the first step toward change.

Satir's philosophy was that the first step toward change is helping people reconnect with themselves through awareness. She believed that self-worth is lessened by blocks to the self such as rules against feelings, rules against seeing what is, rules against asking for what you want, and so forth.

It was her contention that with new awareness comes the release of energy that has been bound up in the blocks to the self and that this energy is necessary for growth and change.

Acceptance of oneself and others is critical to the process of healing.

Satir believed that acceptance of the self, as well as awareness of the self, is necessary for change to take place. She saw non-acceptance as binding-up the energy needed for change. Paradoxically, the acceptance of one's deficits, one's humanness, is necessary before one can move forward to change them.

To her, the essence of wholeness is the acceptance of the self's many parts. She believed that every part of a person, including the dishonest, mean, greedy, etc. parts, have a kernel of needed energy. She would work to help people find a form in which their parts could be acceptable and useful to them.

Satir saw the acceptance of self and others reflected in the ways people communicate, believing that people communicate with themselves as well as others. To her, self-acceptance is reflected by communicating with oneself in nurturing ways. The acceptance of others is reflected by validating the common bond of humanness.

Satir believed that the work of acceptance of oneself and others is the most important personal growth work any therapist can do. She referred to it frequently as becoming more "congruent" or "becoming more fully human."

Acceptance of others, to Satir, meant seeing people as having positive intentions, no matter how horrible their actual behavior. Her approach to working with people was a non-blaming one. Her approach to helping people heal broken relationships was to help them go beyond blaming. She used to say, "People can get stuck in the pain of blame."

Her non-blaming approach was founded on the belief that no one person, event, or factor is ever the total cause of a problem in human interaction. She viewed problems as multi-causal, seeing each member as impacting and being impacted by every other member.

Change is always possible.

Satir believed that much of our behavior is learned. With that premise, she concluded that functional behavior can be learned to take the place of dysfunctional behavior.

She worked on the assumption that when people come for therapy, they want to change even though they may be resistant. She viewed resistance as a natural protection—that it is less threatening to stay with a familiar way of being than risk going into the unknown. She would respect the resistance but ally herself with the part that wanted change.

Satir saw a major part of a therapist's role as helping people know more of their possibilities or choices. She believed that people often resist change because they no longer see themselves as having choices.

The process of change in Satir's view has certain universal stages.

Stage I—*"Status quo"*

> is the beginning stage when people have an awareness of a need for change but the pull to stay with the familiar is stronger than the pull to change.

Stage II—*"Foreign element"*

> is the stage when an event or person such as a therapist enters the system, unbalancing the established dynamics.

Stage III—*"Chaos"*

> is the stage when the system is unbalanced by the impact of the foreign element and people feel out of control, anxious, even ill, aware that their old ways of coping aren't working, but afraid of the unknown; a time of choosing between

reverting back to old familiar ways of coping or taking the risk of learning new ways.

Stage IV—*"New integration"*

is the stage when there is a taking in of new ideas and ways of coping.

Stage V—*"Practice"*

is the final stage when the changes made in the previous stage are reinforced and supported.

This diagram depicts the stages of change:

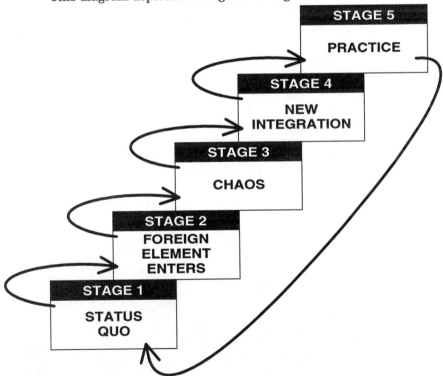

Satir believed that it is important for therapists to understand these universal phases in the process of change so they can recognize them and use them.

She viewed the process of change as never ending. As a consequence, she believed that as people come to understand the process they can more easily reframe the anxiety of the chaos stage into excitement, knowing that they can use their pain to grow and become more integrated.

She used to say, "There is no cure, only evolvement."

OVERVIEW OF SATIR'S PROCESS FOR CHANGE

In order to conceptualize Satir's work, the author has created an artificial construct defining the phases of her work. The phases are a direct reflection of Satir's philosophy and her understanding of the universal phases of change.

In the first two phases, Satir begins to establish rapport and enhance self-worth in order to help people have the strength and the courage to move out of the familiar, out of "status quo." She then works to help people gain awareness and acceptance of themselves so that they can go on to make the needed changes in their lives. Finally, she helps people reinforce their changes by practicing new ways of being.

The phases will be presented here in a linear fashion, each building on the other. This is for the purpose of assisting the reader in understanding Satir's process. In actuality, Satir was organic in her way of working—flowing back and forth between the phases as needed.

Phase I—Making Contact

The first phase of her work is that of "making contact." It was during this time that she would be reaching out and attending to people, in order to establish a connection and enhance each person's sense of being special and unique.

Phase II—Validating

The second phase of her work is that of "validating." In this phase, she would work to enhance self-worth further by letting people know they have value. She did this by reflecting their thoughts and feelings, by appreciating their efforts, by letting them know change was possible, and, in general, by doing whatever she could to enhance their sense of self-worth.

Phase III—Facilitating Awareness

The third phase of her work is that of "facilitating awareness." Here she would work with people to help them gain new awareness of themselves and others. This would include feelings, beliefs, and ways of coping.

Phase IV—Promoting Acceptance

The fourth phase of her work is that of "promoting acceptance." She would work to help people accept their humanness and that of others.

Phase V—Making Changes

The fifth phase of her work is that of "making changes." Having laid the foundation of enhanced self-worth and self-acceptance, she would move on to help people make actual changes in their behavior.

Phase VI—Reinforcing Changes

The sixth and final phase of her work consists of reinforcing the changes made in the previous phase. Here she coached people, guiding them in the practice of their newly acquired skills in order that these might be more fully integrated.

All six of these phases could usually be identified in any single session that Satir conducted. However, as stated earlier, the phases are an artificial construct, something like a road map, in order to help the reader have a conceptual understanding of Satir's process. She would be making contact and validating throughout, flowing back and forth between the phases as necessary in order to follow the processes of her clients.

This diagram depicts Satir's overall process for change:

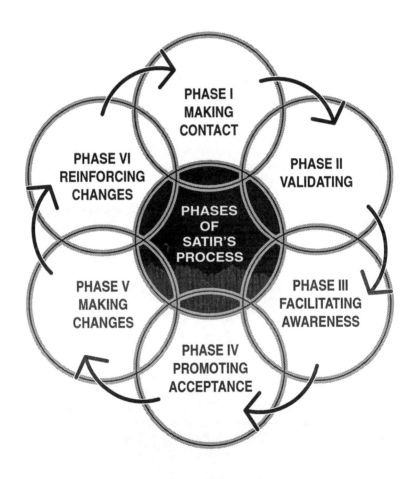

PHASE I
MAKING
CONTACT

PHASE II
VALIDATING

PHASE VI
REINFORCING
CHANGES

PHASES
OF
SATIR'S
PROCESS

PHASE V
MAKING
CHANGES

PHASE III
FACILITATING
AWARENESS

PHASE IV
PROMOTING
ACCEPTANCE

Within each of the phases, Satir applied specific skills to carry out the phase.

The diagram below depicts the phases with their respective skills. Assigning a skill to one particular phase is also an artificial construct for the purpose of promoting understanding. In actual practice Satir may have used the skill in more than one phase, or even all of the phases.

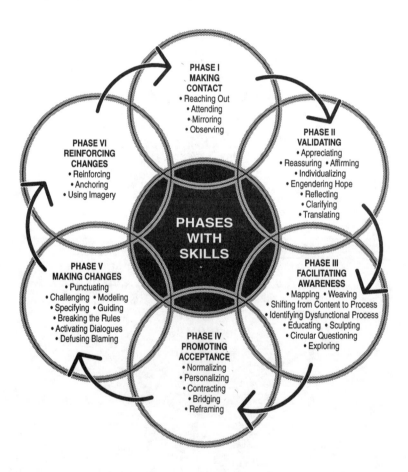

SATIR'S PROCESS FOR CHANGE

Although the skills presented here fit the personality of Satir, a detailed description of the phases of her process and a description of the skills she used for each phase are examined herein—with the hope that the reader will choose from these skills and use them within the context of her own personality and value system.

PHASE I—MAKING CONTACT

Satir began the process of therapy by making contact with people and establishing rapport. In a context of nurturance, she worked to establish a base of trust and a readiness for change.

The skills that Virginia used to do this are *reaching out, attending, mirroring*, and *observing*.

Reaching Out

Satir used her mind, body, and spirit to seek a connection with people. She reached out to people physically, with her hands, eyes, facial expression, and voice tone.

She would usually begin by reaching out and offering to shake hands. Satir believed touch is a basic human need and so she used it extensively as a way of connecting with people.

She would also greet people warmly by learning and using their names. She took her time doing this, making it significant.

She used the position and proximity of her body to reach out as well. When standing, she would usually be facing the person squarely and within arm's length. When sitting, she would often lean in at a 45° angle.

Attending

Satir focused on people individually, giving each person special time and attention in order to make a connection with them. In order to understand them and gain rapport, she listened to them carefully, paying special attention to their words, as well as their voice tone and inflection.

Mirroring

As Satir attended to people, she reflected her belief in their treasurehood through her eyes, facial expression, and touch.

Observing

She attended to people not only to make a connection with them but also in order to observe their body language and process. Because she became totally deaf at the age of five and did not regain her hearing until she was seven, observing was one of her strongest skills.

She observed individuals for changes in their

- eyes;

- facial expression;

- facial skin tone;

- rate and depth of breathing;

- posture;

- distance;

- muscle tone.

She did so in order to be aware of shifts in feelings and in the level of congruence.

She observed couples for their

- individual level of self-worth;

- communication in terms of specificity, directness, openness, clarity, and congruence;

- affection and support for each other;

- handling of differences;

- use of power;

- level of differentiation;

- ways of expressing sexuality;

- decision-making process;

- ability to carry out plans.

She observed families for the

- level of self-worth of each of its members;

- degree of congruence, emotional honesty;

- specificity, directness, and clarity of communication;

- use of defense mechanisms;

- skills at resolving conflict and dealing with anger;

- degree of freedom of expression;

- degree of flexibility, openness to change;

- degree of nurturance, support, and affection;

- level of respect given to each of the members;

- use of power;

- attitudes regarding differences;

- rules;

- acceptance of responsibility;

- appropriateness of roles;

- presence of coalitions;

- presence of splitting, which Satir referred to as the devil/saint syndrome;

- the degree of support for autonomy of its members.*

*See Appendix I for an aid to assessing functionality in families.

PHASE II—VALIDATING

Building upon the foundation begun by the first phase of making contact, Satir added her second phase, validating. She validated people's efforts, their pain, their individuality, their feelings, their wants, and their points of view.

Some of the skills that she used to validate are ***appreciating, reassuring, affirming, individualizing, engendering hope, reflecting, clarifying,*** and ***translating.***

Appreciating

Satir would validate people by verbalizing her appreciation for their pain, efforts, courage, etc.

Examples with individuals:*

> *"I can really appreciate what you have had to cope with."*
>
> *"I can really appreciate the courage you have had to muster."*

Examples with couples:

> *"I can really appreciate the way the two of you have tried to resolve this."*
>
> *"I can appreciate the efforts you both have put into this."*

Examples with families:

> *"I can really appreciate the pain this family has been through."*
>
> *"I can really appreciate the many different ways this family has tried to cope."*

---

*Throughout this book the author has created quotes which exemplify Satir's approach. They are based upon extensive observation of Satir's work.

Reassuring

Satir validated people by conveying her belief to them that they had been doing their best.

Examples with individuals:

> *"At the moment we do something, it's the best we know how to do or we would do something different."*

> *"I believe that at any moment in time, each of us is doing the very best that we can. There may be new information that we can gain, however, which will help us in the future."*

Examples with couples:

> *"You have both been doing the very best with being married that you knew how to do with the models that you had."*

> *"Making mistakes is wonderful because we can look at them and learn and grow."*

Examples with families:

> *"Parenting is probably the most difficult job anyone ever has to do, and yet the only preparation most of us ever had for it was our own parenting. If that left something to be desired, we may not have had everything we needed."*

> *"All of you in this family are doing the very best you can."*

Affirming

Satir validated people by pointing out their assets, good intentions, and positive changes.

Examples with individuals:

> *"Did you know that you could have that much impact on someone?"*

> *"You have feelings, too."*

Examples with couples:

> *"You both had the best of intentions for your marriage."*

> *"Are you aware of the wonderful interaction that just occurred between the two of you?"*

Examples with families:

> *"You parents have good intentions. You want what is best for your children."*

> *"I'm aware of the marvelous way people in this family are being straight with each other. Are you all aware of that?"*

Individualizing

Satir validated people by highlighting their uniqueness and importance.

Examples with couples:

> *"You are each wonderful, unique people with different perspectives. I'm wondering how you see the situation, Theresa?"*

> *"Carl, what is your point of view about how the two of you make decisions?"*

Examples with families:

> *"Well, Jim, each person has his own point of view. Do you agree with your mother's?"*

> *"Mary, George believes that a wife is responsible for seeing to it that the family runs smoothly. What is your belief?"*

> *"Grandma, tell me your name. I know the family calls you, 'Grandma,' but I want to call you by your name."*

> *"Jane, we've heard from everyone else as to what they would like to have happen here. What would you like?"*

Engendering Hope

Satir validated people by helping them regain a sense of hope in their ability to make life better for themselves. She believed that hopelessness drains people of the energy necessary for change.

Examples with individuals:

> *"Although it feels pretty hopeless right now, I see new possibilities for you."*
>
> *"I can understand why you have become discouraged, but I know there are other alternatives we can explore."*

Examples with couples:

> *"I would like to hear from each of you, what you hope to have happen here today?"*
>
> *"I can understand that you both are feeling discouraged about your marriage, but I see lots of possibilities for improving the way you are with each other."*

Examples with families:

> *"After meeting you folks today, I am sure we can work out some ways that this family can have more pleasure and less pain."*
>
> *"I see lots of new possibilities for this family as you learn how to be with each other in different ways."*

Reflecting

Satir validated people by sharing her understanding of their feelings and/or points of view.

Examples with individuals:

> *"I hear that you feel good about the changes going on inside."*

> *"This has turned out to be disappointing for you."*

Examples with couples:

> *"From what you are saying, I'm hearing that you feel pain about what is happening in your marriage."*

> *"Your perception is that you get the brunt of the responsibility in your relationship."*

Examples with families:

> *"I hear that you feel discouraged that your attempts to get good things happening in your family haven't worked."*

> *"You see your mother and father being unhappy with each other."*

Clarifying

Satir validated people by clarifying what they were feeling and/or meaning.

Examples with individuals:

> *"Are you meaning that there is a voice inside that is very critical of you?"*

> *"Is it that you feel stuck because what you have tried hasn't worked?"*

Examples with couples:

> *"Are you saying that you want more freedom in the relationship?"*

> *"I want to check this out. You would like more support from Mary on this. Is that what you are saying?"*

Examples with families:

> *"Do you mean that you are worried that your son isn't saying how he feels?"*

> *"Okay, now let me see if I understand this. You think that a good son is one who always does what he is told. Is that right?"*

Translating

In addition to validating through clarifying, Satir would go beyond this and bring out or translate what she heard the underlying message of the person to be. This often meant "saying the unsayable."

Examples with individuals:

> *"When you say that you are feeling stuck, are you saying that you had hoped to be further along in your career by now?"*

> *"As you tell me that you are unhappy with yourself for your aggressiveness, I'm wondering if you also value that part of you at times?"*

Examples with couples:

> *"I hear you talking about Johnny's problem of wetting the bed and how you don't like the way your husband handles that. Am I also hearing that you are hurting about other things in your relationship with your husband?"*

> *"In addition to your anger regarding the things you've talked about, is there also a part that feels disappointed about what is happening in your marriage right now?"*

Examples with families:

> *"You are telling me that you are very grateful for your father's help since your divorce, but I get the feeling that you don't feel he's allowing you to be an adult. Is anything like that happening for you?*

> *"When you say that your mother makes you do too many things and you don't get time to play football with the guys, are you saying that you feel like her partner rather than her child?"*

PHASE III—FACILITATING AWARENESS

With the establishment of trust through making contact and validating, Satir would begin to move toward change by facilitating awareness.

She focused on facilitating an awareness of family history, of the rules and strengths that had come out of that history, of feelings and behaviors, of dysfunctional processes, and of the parts and/or levels of the self.

Some of the skills that Satir used for facilitating awareness are *mapping, weaving, educating, circular questioning, shifting from content to process, identifying dysfunctional process, sculpting,* and *exploring.*

Mapping

Satir often began the process of facilitating awareness by taking a family history. She referred to this as "mapping."

Mapping involves taking a detailed three-generational history of a person's family, including the birth of his/her grandparents.

The history would include the following:

the birth and death dates for all members including, miscarriages, stillbirths, and abortions;

the historical context of grandparents' and parents' childhoods, such as "The Great Depression";

all major events such as marriages, divorces, moves, natural disasters, and accidents;

the characteristics of each member; and

people of influence unrelated to the family.

When "mapping," Satir would ask for factual data first in order to increase the comfort level. Gradually, she would begin to ask more personal questions about people from the past, such as their characteristics, their beliefs, and their styles of coping.

She used "mapping" to begin to understand the family rules that had been passed down. "Family rules" is her term for the verbal and nonverbal beliefs that families communicate about how people are to be.

Satir looked for rules in such areas as handling money, having fun, being sexual, eating, and handling conflict. She also looked for rules regarding what people could see, hear, feel, think, express, want, and risk.

She identified five rules that are frequently present in dysfunctional families.

- "It's not okay to see and hear what is."

- "It's not okay to feel."

- "It's not okay to say what you think and feel."

- "It's not okay to ask for what you want."

- "It's not okay to take risks."

She used the mapping process as a way of gathering information about rules through observation as well as by questioning. For example, she watched for the expressiveness of the children. It was her belief that children are naturally expressive. If they aren't expressing, they have been stifled by a family rule.

In addition to family rules, Satir also looked for family secrets. With the amount of details that she asked for, secrets would often simply emerge. She believed it is important to bring these secrets out into the open because they further the rules of "it's not okay to see and hear what is" and "it's not okay to say what you think and feel."

Examples of Questions During Mapping:

Regarding Historical Data

> *"Do you know when your grandfather was born? If not, when do you think it might have been? Where was he born? Are you aware of what life was like at the time of his birth? Are you aware of the family situation in the family he was born into? Is he still living? What did he die of? When did he die?"*

Regarding Major Events

> *"When were your parents married? Do you know how they met? What do you know about their courtship? What is the status of their marriage now?"*

Regarding Characteristics

> *"If you were to send me to the airport to pick up your grandmother, how would I know her? Give me some adjectives that would describe her personality. How do you feel about these characteristics, positively or negatively?"*

Regarding Rules

> *"What would your mother have said about money?"*

> *"How did your parents deal with differences?"*

Regarding Secrets

> *"What is your birthdate? . . . I see that your parents were married on a date that is less than nine months before your birth. Are you aware of what the circumstances were?"*

Regarding People of Influence

> *"Were there others outside your family who were influential in your growing up?"*

Weaving

Satir would weave back and forth between family history and current interactions in order to create a sense of distance and safety, as well as to gain important historical information.

Examples with individuals:

> *"How did your parents have fun? How about your grandparents? How do you have fun?"* (Weaving back to the past, then into the present.)

> *"You are saying that you are struggling with who you are sexually? Tell me, how did your mother express her sexuality?"* (Weaving from the present back to the past.)

Examples with couples:*

> *"We have a difference between the two of you about who is supposed to do what. Let's take a look at each of your histories and see how that came to be."*

> *"Jim, you seem to be in a lot of pain right now about what is going on between you and your wife. I have a hunch that we can help you with that if we do a little digging into the past. Are you willing to do that with me?"*

Examples with families:

> *"I'm hearing that Dad remembers a lot of fun times when he was growing up, but Mom's family was more serious. So what does this family do for fun?"*

> *"So this family is struggling with how to deal with conflict. Since we learn how to deal with conflict from our models, let's take a look back at your models, Mom and Dad, and see what we can learn."*

*See Appendix II for a questionnaire designed to aid in the exploration of family histories with couples.

Educating

Satir believed that when people get new information, they have new possibilities.

Because of this, she would frequently offer information regarding the universal principles of human process. She usually did this quite casually, which seemed to help people accept the information more easily.

Examples with individuals:

> *"There are always choices, so let's look at yours in this situation."*

> *"Within us are many wonderful resources like breathing, so how about taking a deep breath right now in order to help those butterflies."*

Examples with couples:

> *"People can't see their own backsides, so tell your wife how you see her being with your daughter."*

> *"Communication is to relationships what breath is to life, so let's see if we can help the two of you talk to each other."*

Examples with families:

> *"You can go a little closer to your mother, nothing terrible will happen!"*

> *"We learn from our models, so let's take a look at how your parents parented."*

Circular Questioning

Satir worked to create awareness of current process by asking one person her observations of the interaction of two others. This type of questioning can be defined as circular because the focus is on information about the interaction of others, as opposed to information about the self.

When using circular questioning, Satir was operating from her model of seeing families as made up of triangles. She looked at those in the triangle as having three roles, that of a responder, an activator, and an observer. She would use this concept by asking one person to take on the role of observer and report what they saw happening in the interaction between the other two, the activator and the responder.

Examples with individuals:

> *"Joey, can you give me a picture of how you see your brother and dad getting along?"*

> *"Martha, as you think about how your parents deal with conflict, how would you describe their interaction?"*

Examples with couples:

> *"Manuel, how would you describe the relationship between your wife and her mother?"*

> *"Margarita, how do you see your new husband relating to your children?"*

Examples with families:

> *"Suzy, what do you see Mommy and Daddy doing when they aren't happy with each other?"*

> *"Carol, how do you see your son and husband being with each other right now?"*

Shifting From Content to Process

Satir often stated that "the problem is never the problem, it is the coping with the problem that is the problem."

Understanding that people naturally focus on the problem, however, Satir developed a method for helping shift their focus onto coping. She did this by guiding them to explore the "how," as opposed to the "what," of situations.

Examples with individuals:

> *"So you are feeling scared about speaking up? How are you scaring yourself?"*

> *"How are you talking to yourself right now that is making you feel bad about yourself?"*

Examples with couples:

> *"I hear a lot of pain in your relationship as you each tell me your side of the story. Since we learn from our models, I am interested to know how each of your parents handled their differences."*

> *"You both have been sharing your disappointment over your son's truancy. I'm wondering how you have talked with each other about your pain?"*

Examples with families:

> *"Charles, you are feeling frustrated because Jeff doesn't seem to be motivated. Do you know what makes Jeff happy? How do people in this family find out what makes other people happy?"*

> *"You have a different opinion on this matter than your mother. How do people in this family disagree with each other?"*

Identifying Dysfunctional Process

Once Satir had successfully shifted the focus off content and onto process in a specific situation, she worked to help people gain awareness of the specific dysfunctional process occurring. She believed that most people are not aware of their own process and need help to see how they are functioning. She used to say "we cannot see our own back sides."

Examples with an individual:

> *"What I'm hearing, Steve, is that you make a promise to yourself and then you don't deliver to yourself? Is that what you are struggling with?"*

> *"So what goes on for you, Maria, is that you think that your husband is too hard on the kids, but you can't tell him. Is that the way it is—that you might get in trouble with him if you did?"*

Examples with couples:

> *"What I see happening between the two of you is that you are each feeling pain about what is happening in your relationship, but you show it differently. You, John, have become silent and withdrawn. You, Joan, have learned to reach out to the kids instead of to John. You both want more closeness, but don't know how to make that happen. Does that ring true for each of you?"*

> *"My sense is that the two of you had high hopes for your relationship that have not come true and that it hasn't been okay to talk about those disappointments. Is that a possibility?"*

Examples with families:*

> *"One of the things that is coming to me as we talk is that this*

family doesn't know how to find out what makes other people happy. Could that be?"

"As you tell me what a typical day is like in this family, I get the feeling that people are real hungry for contact, but they don't know how to go about getting it. Does that seem to fit?"

*See Appendix I for an aid to assessing family functionality.

Sculpting

Satir created sculpting as another way of facilitating awareness and altering perceptions. Sculpting involved the placement of people in relationship to each other in such a way that it revealed the essence of their emotional relationships.

She used sculpting in two different ways. One was to share what she observed. The other was to elicit information and feelings from others.

Sculpting for Sharing Observations

When Satir wanted to share an observation, she would either use her communication stances to depict dysfunctional coping mechanisms, or create positions, on the spot, that seemed to reflect the situation.

The communication stances demonstrated what she believed to be four of the most common dysfunctional coping mechanisms used under stress: placating, blaming, being super-reasonable, and being irrelevant.

Examples of using the communication stances:

Example 1

> She would ask a person to get down on one knee in a begging position, looking up and repeating, "It's all my fault, I'm so sorry," demonstrating the placating position.

Example 2

> She would ask a person to put one hand on a hip and point a blaming finger with the other hand, while repeating, "It's all your fault," several times, demonstrating the blaming position.

Example 3

She would ask a person to stand "at attention" military style, making no eye contact, being very intellectual, and repeating something like "one makes errors, that is the human condition," demonstrating the super-reasonable position.

Example 4

She would ask a person to escape by walking off-balance and being unfocused in conversation, in order to demonstrate the irrelevant position.

After placing people in these stances, Satir would ask them to freeze and hold, heightening the body's experience of the position. She would then ask what they had experienced in terms of body sensations and feelings.

Satir used these communication stances at times when she perceived an overuse of a communication style. She understood, however, that there are times when pleasing, using one's head, or escaping, are very appropriate and healthy responses.

Examples of creating personalized, on the spot, sculpts:

Example 1

"As I have listened to you two talk about your relationship, I have gained a picture that I would like to share with you."

Example 2

"I have a picture of what it is like to be living in this family. Let me show you."

Sculpting to Elicit Information and Feelings:

Examples with individuals:

Example 1

> *"As you look at me now from this kneeling position, what is that like for you?"*

Example 2

> *"I noticed your voice loud and your finger pointed straight at the other person. Is that action familiar to you?"*

Examples with couples:

Example 1

> *"I think it might be helpful if each of you shared your picture of your relationship. What I would like for you to do is show me without using words. Place your partner and yourself in relation to each other the way you experience the relationship. You can be standing, sitting, kneeling, facing toward, facing away, close, distant, whatever will express how you experience the relationship."*

Example 2

> *"Donald, I see that it is difficult for you to find words to express yourself in terms of how you feel about your relationship with your wife. That's okay because we can express ourselves in many different ways. How about if you place your wife and yourself in relation to each other in a way that reflects how you see the relationship?"*

Examples with families:

Example 1

> *"I would be very interested in seeing how each of you experience your family. Come, Joe, make a picture of how you see the members of your family relating to each other. Place each person as you see them in relation to the rest."* (Satir would then ask what each member was feeling personally and feeling regarding the others.)

Example 2

> *"It would be helpful to me to get a picture of what it's like at the dinner table with your family. How about if you each take your places as if you were around the table at home and then show me what happens. Who talks, who is silent, who talks to whom, that kind of thing?"*

Examples using a group:

Example 1

> *"Linda, you are giving me a picture of how you are experiencing your responsibilities at work and I would like to share that with you. I would like for you to pick out three people from the group to be your employees. Then I would like for each of them to come up and hang on you in some way."*

> *"Okay, now that they are all hanging all over you, Linda, how do you feel?"*

Example 2

"Juan, I'm hearing that you have something going on regarding your family that might be helpful for us to take a look at. Pick out people from the group to be your mother, father, sister, and a stand-in for yourself."

"Now place your parents in such a way as to show how you see them being with each other. Then place your stand-in and your sister in the picture with your parents, positioning each of you as you experience it in your family."

"Okay, everyone freeze in those positions. How is that for you seeing your family in this way, Juan?" (Satir might also ask Juan's stand-in to leave and ask Juan, himself, to go into the sculpt in order to elicit even more of his feelings.)

Satir's use of sculpting reflected two important principles of her work. First, that action facilitates the process of change. She got people moving to help them break out of their old patterns by having new perceptions as a result of different experiences.

Secondly, she knew that the body carries universal feelings and wisdom within which can often be elicited through sculpting. She used to say, "The body doesn't lie!"

Exploring

Satir created awareness by helping people explore and understand the different parts or levels of themselves.*

She touched on perceptions, interpretations, feelings, and the levels below feelings, such as feelings about feelings, beliefs, expectations, wants, hopes, and yearnings. (She did this with great sensitivity, going only as far as a person could accept.)

The levels of the self can be thought of as an iceberg with the tip of the iceberg representing the visible behaviors and all the other levels effecting the behavior being below the surface.

Exploring Perceptions

Examples with individuals:

> *"How do you see yourself being with your boss?"*

> *"What is your perception of yourself as look in the mirror?"*

Examples with couples:

> *"As you listen to your partner, what are you hearing going on with him?"*

> *"What do you see as you look at his expression?"*

Examples with families:

> *"As your son speaks to you, what are you hearing him say?"*

> *"What are you seeing as you watch your daughter and son talk with each other?*

---

*The concept of the levels of the self was presented by John Banmen at Module II Satir Training, Crested Butte, Colorado, July 1987.

Exploring Interpretations

Examples with individuals:

> *"What interpretation are you giving to this situation that is causing you to feel bad?"*
>
> *"How are you interpreting this situation to mean that you don't fit in?"*

Examples with couples:

> *"As you look at your husband's face, what meaning do you give to what you see?"*
>
> *"How do you interpret your wife's statement that she needs more of your time?"*

Examples with families:

> *"When your mother says she wants the family to be closer, what does that mean to you? How do you interpret that?"*
>
> *"I'm aware that you have been listening intently to your father. How do you interpret what you are hearing?"*

Exploring Projections (Shadows)

Satir often took her exploration of interpretations beyond the examples described above when she suspected that the interpretations were based on projections or, as she called them, "shadows." She defined shadows as the feelings we have about significant individuals in our lives that we inappropriately assign to other individuals.

Exploring Projections

Example with couples:

Dialogue 1

> Virginia— *"As you hear your husband's voice, what is happening for you, Mary?"*
>
> Mary— *"I'm feeling very frightened."*
>
> Virginia— *"What is frightening you?"*
>
> Mary— *"He sounds angry with me."*
>
> Virginia— *"That frightens you?"*
>
> Mary— *"Yes."*
>
> Virginia— *"How does that frighten you?"*
>
> Mary— *"I guess I'm afraid he's going to hurt me."*
>
> Virginia— *"Has he ever done that?"*
>
> Mary— *"No."*
>
> Virginia— *"What do you think the fear is about then?"*
>
> Mary— *"Well, when I was little and my dad got angry, he would often lose control and hurt my mother."*
>
> Virginia— *"So you have carried that fear over to your husband."*
>
> Mary— *"Yes, I guess I have because my husband has never done anything to indicate he would hurt me."*

Exploring Projections

Example with couples:

Dialogue 2

Virginia— *"David, you are saying that you are experiencing your wife as controlling. What is she doing that you are experiencing as controlling?"*

David— *"She is telling me that she wants me to cancel my appointment with a friend for Friday night."*

Virginia— *"You don't like being put in that position."*

David— *"No, I don't."*

Virginia— *"I'm gathering that the feeling of not liking to be controlled is a strong one for you."*

David— *"Yes, it is."*

Virginia— *"Is this something you have experienced before?"*

David— *"Yes. My mother was very controlling. When I was sixteen, she told me I had to join her church. I ran away instead."*

Virginia— *"Is it possible that some of that feeling is still with you in relation to this issue with your wife?"*

David— *"I suppose so. I really get bent out of shape when my wife tells me to do something."*

Exploring Projections

Example with families:

Dialogue 1

Kim— *"Rick defies me all the time! He and his father are just alike."*

Virginia— *"When your son says 'no' to you, you see him as being like his father."*

Kim— *"Yes, they are both stubborn."*

Virginia— *"How do you experience your husband as being stubborn?"*

Kim— *"Well, when he gets something in his head, he won't change his mind."*

Virginia— *"That's frustrating."*

Kim— *"Yes, very."*

Virginia— *"Are there times when Rick is cooperative as well?"*

Kim— *"Yes."*

Virginia— *"We all put feelings on people that don't belong to them from time to time. I'm wondering if your feeling of frustration has more to do with your relationship with your husband than with Rick."*

Kim— *"That's a possibility."*

Exploring Projections

Example with families:

Dialogue 2

Michael— *"See how my son is being here, not looking at me or talking to me. This is the way he is most of the time. He seems to not want me around."*

Virginia— *"How is that for you?"*

Michael— *"I feel rejected."*

Virginia— *"You interpret his behavior as directed at you."*

Michael— *"Yes, I do."*

Virginia— *"Is it possible that there are other reasons for his behavior?"*

Michael— *"I guess so."*

Virginia— *"Was there an earlier time in your life when you experienced rejection?"*

Michael— *"Yes, by my father. He didn't like me."*

Virginia— *"Could it be that those feelings are being carried over to your interpretations of your son's behavior?"*

Michael— *"I never looked at it that way."*

Exploring Feelings

Satir continually explored for feelings—monitoring words and shifts in body language.

Examples with individuals:

> *"What are you feeling at this moment?"*

> *"Go inside and tell me what you are feeling."*

(If a person could not identify feelings, Satir would ask questions to help her. "Where do you sense that in your body? Is there any part of your body that you are aware of at this moment? Any tightness that you are aware of?" She would also encourage the person to breathe with eyes closed to see if any image emerged. If so, Satir would explore the image in order to determine the feelings connected with it.)

Examples with couples:

> *"How are you feeling as you hear your husband talk about his pain?"*

> *"As you get in touch with the expectations carried into the marriage, how are you feeling?"*

Examples with families:

> *"Now that you are aware of this new picture of your father, what are you feeling?"*

> *"How do you feel as you watch your husband and son share with each other?"*

Exploring Feelings About Feelings

Exploring feelings about feelings often revealed beliefs against having certain feelings.

Examples with individuals:

> *"How do you feel about feeling relieved?"*

> *"How is that for you, being frightened?"*

Examples with couples:

> *"As you get in touch with your disappointment about the relationship, how do you feel?"*

> *"As you feel close now toward your partner, how does that make you feel?"*

Examples with families:

> *"You are angry with your mother about this. How is it for you to be angry with your mother?"*

> *"Being aware of the sadness you feel about the distance between you and your son, Jesse, how do you feel about feeling sad?"*

Exploring Expectations

With individuals:

> *"What did you expect of yourself in relation to getting angry?"*

> *"Do you expect yourself to do it perfectly every time?"*

With couples:

> *"What were your expectations for a husband, Jean?"*

> *"John, as you think back, what did you expect of a wife?"*

With families:

> *"Harry, when you were told that you were going to be the father of a little girl, what did you expect that would be like?"*

> *"Bob, what did you expect life would be like, coming into a ready-made family?"*

*Exploring Beliefs**

Examples with individuals:

> *"It sounds like you believe it's dangerous to ask for what you want. Is that so?"*

> *"Do you believe you have a choice in this situation?"*

Examples with couples:

> *"I hear you believing that your wife doesn't love you if she differs with you on this. Is that what you are saying to yourself?"*

> *"Is it your belief that your husband should know how you want to be cared for without you having to tell him?"*

Examples with families:

> *"Muriel, what do you believe will happen if you share your feelings with your mother?"*

> *"Terry, as you express concern regarding your son's adverturous nature, I'm wondering if you believe the world is a dangerous place?"*

In addition to direct exploration for the beliefs or rules of a family, Virginia often explored for them indirectly. She did this by asking how the family dealt with critical areas such as angry feelings and conflict.

> *"I'm wondering how people in this family let each other know when they are angry?"*

> *"Janey, what happens in this family when people don't agree?"*

*See Appendix III for a list of commonly held dysfunctional beliefs.

Exploring Wants

Examples with individuals:

> *"What are you wanting from yourself in this regard?"*

> *"I hear you wanting more time for yourself. Is that true?"*

Examples with couples:

> *"What do you want from your husband when he is home?"*

> *"Do you want more verbal support from your wife—is that what you are saying?"*

Examples with families:

> *"What one specific thing do you want from your stepfather?"*

> *"What is it that you want out of your relationship with your adult daughter?"*

Exploring Hopes

Examples with individuals:

> *"And what do you hope will happen for you here today, Susan?"*

> *"What is your hope for you, Kevin, as you see yourself five years from now?"*

Examples with couples:

> *"When you thought about marrying, Karen, what did you hope your husband would be like?"*

> *"Joe, you had high hopes when you proposed to Karen. What were those hopes?"*

Examples with families:

> *"When you learned you were having a son, Willie, what did you hope he would be like?"*

> *"As you see your parents get back together, Justine, what do you hope will happen for your family?"*

Exploring Yearnings*

Yearnings can be thought of as being at the deepest level of the self. Satir explored for yearnings in order to help people bring them into awareness and gain acceptance of them as part of one's humanness.

Examples with individuals:

> *"You feel angry with your mother because she repeatedly disappoints you. What is it that you long for from your mother?"*

> *"You look pained as you talk about feeling your father's disapproval of you. Is there a yearning inside for his approval?"*

Examples with couples:

> *"Susan, as you experience the feeling of being abandoned by your husband, are you aware of any longing as a child for your father to be there for you?"*

> *"Rick, as you express your disappointment at not being recognized for your talents and efforts in your marriage, I'm wondering if there has been a yearning within you for recognition that began even before you were married?"*

Examples with families:

> *"Margaret, as I hear you sharing here with your family about your mother and the children's grandmother, I have the strong sense that you long for her acceptance. Does that fit at all?"*

> *"As you hear your son expressing a desire to have more of your undivided attention, Paul, does this feel familiar? Was this something you longed for from your father?"*

*See Appendix III for a list of commonly held unmet yearnings.

PHASE IV—PROMOTING ACCEPTANCE

Satir's work reflected a belief that acceptance of the self and of others is one of the keys to healing. It is not only necessary for enhancing self-worth but also for creating a foundation from which change could occur.

Some of the skills that she used to promote acceptance are **normalizing**, **personalizing**, **contracting**, **bridging**, and **reframing**.

Normalizing

Satir validated people by letting them know that their feelings were normal and human. (She often did this with humor.)

Examples with individuals:

> *"Making mistakes is part of being human. Mistakes give us information for our learning and growing."*

> *"So you see yourself as being chunky. I know something about that!" (She says with humor.)*

Examples with couples:

> *"You are now aware that part of you wanted to get married for security. Well, that's par for the course!"*

> *All couples will go through disappointment after marriage, I'm wondering how the two of you have coped with that?"*

Examples with families:

> *"Does anyone else in this family, besides Keith, know about being afraid to say what they feel?"*

> *"I think all of us growing up have had to deal with the struggle in our teen years that you are going through, Roberto."*

Personalizing

When Satir saw people assigning responsibility for their pain to causes outside themselves, she would shift the focus back to the person. This is empowering because people can only change themselves, not others.

Examples with individuals:

> *"I hear your frustration and I'm wondering what you are saying to yourself that is keeping you frustrated?"*

> *"Oscar, how are you allowing your distractions to keep you from your promise to yourself to do the dishes?"*

Examples with couples:

> *"You see your husband as being 'wimpy.' I'm gathering from what you said earlier that you might know something about that yourself. Is that true?"*

> *"As you speak, I'm hearing you talk about what you think your wife wants; but what about you, what do you want, Harry?"*

Examples with families:

> *"This really doesn't have much to do with your mother, Kathryn. It has to do with you. You know that, don't you?"*

> *"You fear that your children don't know how to stand up for themselves. Is that true for you as well?"*

Contracting

Satir would engage people by asking about their willingness to hear new information or try on a new behavior. She would, in essence, establish a contract with them.

Examples with individuals:

> *I have a picture of what I think is happening for you. Would you like to hear it?"*

> *"Would you be willing to accept that placating helped you survive, but now it is hindering you?"*

Examples with couples:

> *"I am picking up that you don't know what makes your husband happy. Would you like to hear from him what makes him happy?"*

> *"You have been in a blaming place with each other and it hasn't worked. Are you willing to make some changes in your way of being with each other?"*

Examples with families:

> *"I see a picture of what is happening in this family that is causing pain. Do you want to know about my picture?"* (She would then sculpt her picture of their relationships with each other.)

> *"I think people in this family feel misunderstood. I have some ideas about how this is happening. Would you like to hear them?"* (She would ask each member separately so she had the individual involvement and commitment of each.)

Bridging

. Virginia worked to promote not only self-acceptance but also acceptance between people. One of the ways she did this was by identifying similar feelings or values between those who were in conflict.

Examples with individuals:

> *"So, Maria, I'm hearing that you can identify with the feeling of isolation that your daughter has expressed. You had similar feelings in high school."*

> *"As you connect with your father's determination, is that something that you know about as well?"*

Examples with couples:

> *"So you both value time together. You simply differ on how to use that time."*

> *"I'm hearing that there is a strong commitment on the part of each of you to this relationship."*

Example with a family:

Dialogue 1

Father— *"Steve acts like he's not a part of our family anymore. When he's home he's either in his room listening to music or on the phone to some girl. I don't understand why he doesn't spend time with us."*

Virginia— *"Well, let's see, Steve is seventeen. What do you remember about your interests when you were seventeen?"*

Father—   *"Cars and girls."*

Virginia—   *"So you know something about where he's coming from."*

Example with a family:

Dialogue 2

Virginia—   *"Dad, what do you want for your son as he approaches manhood?"*

Father—   *"I want him to be a responsible person who can provide for his family. That's why I get on him when he's being irresponsible around the house."*

Virginia—   *"Mom, what do you want for your son as he approaches manhood?"*

Mother—   *"I want him to be a good father and husband, but I don't think yelling at him for not doing his chores is the way to deal with him."*

Virginia—   *"So you both want the same thing for your son but differ on how to go about helping him."*

Reframing

In order to further acceptance, Satir often turned something that was thought of negatively into something that could be seen positively.

Examples with individuals:

> *"You call yourself stubborn. In what areas of your life do you think your tenaciousness has helped you?"*
>
> *"Would you be willing to consider that there are times when you need your dishonest part?"*

Examples with couples:

> *"So your husband has a highly developed skill in this area."* (The wife had been complaining about her husband's criticism of her.)
>
> *"I'm hearing that the two of you both know a lot about getting your needs met."* (Both partners had been accusing each other of being selfish.)

Examples with families:

> *"I see the members of this family know a great deal about standing firm."* (Reframing a power struggle.)
>
> *"Jerry, what are you experiencing as you see your son learning how to become a man and stand on his own two feet?"* (Reframing son's acting out behavior as a part of a developmental task.)

PHASE V—MAKING CHANGES

After facilitating greater awareness and acceptance, Satir would move into the crucial phase of "making changes." Here is where she could be firm. She would ally herself with the parts that desired growth, and work relentlessly to get people beyond their defenses so change could occur.

Some of the skills she used during this phase are *punctuating, challenging, modeling, specifying, guiding, breaking the rules, activating dialogues, defusing blaming,* and *differentiating.*

Punctuating

Satir would intervene to stop what she observed to be dysfunctional process, whether with individuals regarding their intrapersonal processes or whether with couples or families regarding their interpersonal process.

Examples with individuals:

> *"Now just wait a minute here, Barbara. Do you really believe your mother didn't bathe you until you were six years old?"*

> *"Hold on, Jim, let's take a look at that expectation."*

Examples with couples:

> *"Wait, Shirley, use 'I' instead of 'we.' Speak for yourself."*

> *"Okay, let's stop for a moment. I would like to share what I see happening here with you two."*

Examples with families:

> *"Let's see if we can make something different happen here."*

> *"Okay, so now that we know what the pain has been about, let's work on getting some better things happening in this family."*

Challenging

Satir would challenge people to make changes. This could be in terms of dysfunctional perceptions, interpretations, beliefs, expectations, or behaviors.

Examples with individuals:

> *"Is it true that you must always be nice? Are there times when it would be okay to be other than nice?"*

> *"Are you ready to start a new process for yourself?"*

Examples with couples:

> *"Now that you see that you have put an expectation on your spouse that doesn't fit, are you willing to let go of that?"*

> *"Do you really think that if you tell your wife what's going on for you, she will disintegrate?"*

Examples with families:

> *"As you look at your daughter, are you willing to say to her what is in your heart?"*

> *"Would you be willing, Jeff, to tell your father what it was like for you when he left the family?"*

Modeling

Satir used herself as a model for people. She demonstrated being congruent, clear, specific, direct and open in the way she communicated with people.

Examples with individuals:

> *"You know, Myra, I am getting the feeling that something is not right between us. Are there feelings that you are having that you feel unsafe to talk about?"*

> *"What I see, Frank, is that it is very hard for you to let go of the hurt."*

Examples with couples:

> *"I see that each of you has inside pain that is coming out in the relationship in hurtful ways."*

> *"So let's get clear here. What would each of you like to have happen in your relationship?"*

Examples with families:

> *"I'm hearing that Mom's drinking is a problem for this family. Is that true?"*

> *"I believe that even though Dad isn't living with the family now, his presence is being felt very strongly."*

Specifying

As a part of making changes, Satir would help people speak more concretely. She would challenge them to get more specific.

Examples with individuals:

> *"You are saying that you don't see yourself going anywhere? Can you be more specific. What do you mean by 'not going anywhere'?"*

> *"You are encouraged by your progress. What specifically are you doing that is pleasing you?"*

Examples with couples:

> *"You are saying that you want more involvement from your husband. What does more involvement mean to you?"*

> *"You don't like the way your wife is looking at you. Tell me what you see."*

Examples with families:

> *"So you are unhappy with the children's behavior. Tell me, what are the behaviors that are bothering you?"*

> *"What exactly do you want from your husband when it comes to helping out with the discipline?"*

Guiding

In addition to modeling effective ways of being, Satir would give people specific guidance on how to make changes.

Examples with individuals:

> *"As you imagine yourself with your boss now, see yourself breathing and keeping centered."*

> *"Talk to me. Tell me those things that have been stuck in your craw from your childhood experience of your mother."*

Examples with couples:

> *"Let's check that out, Betty, and see if that really is what your partner is thinking. Turn toward him and ask him if that's what he's thinking."*

> *"Share with Mario what you feel about him as your husband, because I'm getting that you feel many wonderful things that he never hears."*

Examples with families:

> *"Turn toward your son and tell him that it's okay for him to feel differently about his daddy than you do, because that is what you just said you want him to know."*

> *"Why don't you pull your chair up so you can be close to your daughter for a moment and let her know about those good feelings for her that you are telling me about."*

Breaking The Rules

Satir would facilitate change by creating behavioral experiences for people that would help them break their dysfunctional family rules automatically.

Examples with individuals:

> *"What are you feeling?"* (Breaking the rule that it's not okay to feel.)

> *"So everyone in your family knew that Dad was not faithful to your mother, but no one talked about it. Is that right?"* (Breaking the rule that it's not okay to talk about the family secret.)

Examples with couples:

> *"Would you be willing to risk telling your husband what you want from him?"* (Breaking the rules not to ask for what you want and not to take risks.)

> *"You look like you have been having strong feelings while your wife was talking. Can you put words to them?"* (Breaking the rules not to feel and not to say what you feel.)

Examples with families:

> *"What would you like to say to your mother as you see her position in this sculpt?"* (Breaking the rule not to say what you are thinking and/or feeling.)

> *"What do you see as you look at this sculpt."* (Breaking the rule not to see and not to say what you see.)

Activating Dialogues

In bringing about changes in communication patterns, Satir would often create dialogues between people. She would position them so that they were facing each other squarely and almost knee to knee.

Examples with couples:

Example 1

> *"Mary, how about it if you take both of your husband's hands and look into his eyes and tell him those wonderful things that you just said to me about him?"*
>
> *"Now, Ted, how is that for you to hear these things from Mary?"*

Example 2

> *"Joe, can you pull up your chair here a little and turn toward your wife? Tell her what your pain is about."*

Examples with families:

Example 1

> *"Joe and Mike, I'd like for you to bring your chairs up close and face each other. Now, Joe, would you tell your son what you started to share with me about how you miss him?"*
>
> *"Mike, what is happening inside of you as you hear your dad say that he misses you?"*

Example 2

> *"Joyce, I think it might be helpful for your mother to hear what you are thinking and feeling, so just move yourself so you can look at her and tell her."*

> *"Linda, as you heard what your daughter had to say, what feelings came up for you?"*

Defusing Blaming

Satir worked to defuse blaming by shifting the focus from the person being blamed to the process.

Examples of defusing blaming between a couple:

Dialogue 1

Carla— *"Ken never listens to me. See how he's ignoring me right now."*

Virginia— *"What behaviors do you see that tell you he's not listening?"* (Beginning to differentiate behaviors from interpretations.)

Carla— *"He's looking at the ceiling."*

Virginia— *"What else do you see that tells you he's not listening?"* (Continuing to differentiate behaviors.)

Carla— *"His facial expression."*

Virginia— *"What do you see going on in his face that says to you he's not listening?"* (Continuing to differentiate behaviors.)

Carla— *"Well, just the way he's looking."*

Virginia— *"What interpretation are you giving to your perception?"* (Personalizing by exploring for interpretations; also educating.)

Carla— *"That he really doesn't want to hear me. That he really doesn't care."*

Virginia— *"Okay, that is one possible interpretation. Are*

you open to any others?" (Affirming and contracting.)

Carla— *"Yes."*

Virginia— *"Ken, tell me. From your perspective, what are you aware of? What was going on with you?"*

Ken— *"Do you want to know the truth?"*

Virginia— *"Yes."*

Ken— *"I was thinking about a deadline I have at work."*

Virginia— *"Was there any part of you that was feeling upset with Carla?"*

Ken— *"I don't think so. I probably wasn't listening, she's right, but it wasn't because I don't care. I do care. I am just preoccupied about this deadline."*

Virginia— *"How are you feeling right now, Carla?"*

Carla— *"Better. I didn't realize that he was so worried about the deadline."*

Dialogue 2

Mary— (To husband.) *"You are irresponsible, Tom. You always make promises and then you don't keep them. You are hopeless."*

Virginia— *"Mary, I want you to turn toward me and just talk to me right now."*

(Turning to Tom.) *"Tom, I will get back to you."*

Virginia— (turning back to Mary) *"Mary, you sound very disappointed."* (Shifting to the level of her softer feelings.)

Mary— *"Yes, I am terribly disappointed. I thought Tom would change, but he's still the same."*

Virginia— *"You had an expectation that he would be different than you are experiencing him."* (Shifting to Mary's expectation.)

Mary— *"Yes, I can't believe he's so irresponsible?"*

Virginia— *"What are your feelings at this moment?"*

Mary— *"Hurt. This isn't the way I wanted it."*

Virginia— *"So you had a picture in your head of how your partner was supposed to be."*

Mary— *"I guess so. My dad was irresponsible and I swore to myself that I would never get involved with an irresponsible man."*

Virginia— *"How did it feel when your dad didn't keep his promises?"*

Mary— *"Terrible. I thought he must not love me."*

Virginia— *"When we are children we try to make sense out of things. Do you suppose you decided that the reason your dad didn't keep his promise was because you weren't lovable?"* (Shifting to her underlying belief.)

Mary— *"Uh-huh."*

Virginia— *"With your knowledge now as an adult about*

your dad's struggle with alcoholism, would you be willing to consider that when he broke a promise to you, it had to do with him and not with you?" (Challenging her belief.)

Mary— *"Yes."*

Virginia— *"How are you feeling right now?"* (Anchoring her change.)

Mary— *"Relief."*

Virginia— *"Would you be willing to turn toward Tom and look at him, and see if there is anything of your father's that you have put on Tom?"* (Exploring for a projection.)

Mary— *"I guess his irresponsibleness."*

Virginia— *"Would you be willing to image your father sitting beside Tom and then see yourself taking the label of 'irresponsible' off Tom and giving it back to your father?"* (Identifying the projection and challenging her to let go of it.)

Mary— *"Okay, I did it."*

Virginia— *"How are you feeling right now?"* (Anchoring another change.)

Mary— *"Good."*

Virginia— *"Okay. Now I would like to check in with Tom and see what this has been like for him."*

As Satir worked with Mary, she by-passed Mary's anger and concentrated on her underlying feelings of disappointment and hurt. She then led Mary to an awareness and acceptance of her expectations and beliefs. Once there was acceptance, Satir challenged the belief and helped her let go of it. Finally, she shifted the focus back to the present and to Mary's relationship with her partner—helping her to perceive him more realistically.

She then shifted to Tom, defusing his blaming by eliciting his expectations, beliefs and yearnings.

Virginia— *"Well, Tom, how has this been for you?"*

Tom— *"Very interesting. I had no idea that Mary was putting stuff on me that belonged to her father. She's always raggin' on me about something! She forgets the things I do right. I can do everything I'm supposed to do for a week and then forget one little thing and she's yelling at me. She's a complete nag!"*

Virginia— *"You expect her to appreciate what you do?"* (Shifting to his expectation.)

Tom— *"Yeah. Wouldn't you? I give up. You can't please women!"*

Virginia— *"You have decided that it's impossible to please any woman."* (Shifting to his belief.)

Tom— *"Well, I haven't been able to please either of my wives and I certainly was never able to please my mother. She was on my back all of the time. She never gave me credit for anything."*

Virginia— *"Your experience with women has not been good. You have really wanted some recognition."* (Shifting to his wants.)

Tom—   *"Sure, who wouldn't?*

Virginia—   *"You have yearned for recognition from women for a long time."* (Shifting to his yearning.)

Tom—   *"Yes, I have."*

Virginia—   *"What choices do you see for getting some of that yearning for recognition met with Mary?"*

Tom—   *"I don't know."*

Virginia—   *"How about asking Mary if she would be willing to let you know when she appreciates something you have done? I don't know what she will say, but you can ask."* (Guiding him to a new, healthier way of coping.)

Tom—   *"Okay."*

Examples of defusing blaming within a family:

Dialogue 1

Lynn—   (Mother) *"Jim is much too hard on the kids. They commit a misdemeanor and they get punished for a felony!"*

Virginia—   *"Now, let me see here. Jim is the children's stepfather, is that right?"* (Shifts focus to facts.)

Lynn—   *"Yes, that's right."*

Virginia—   *"And how long have you been married?"* (Keeping the focus off the accused and onto facts.)

Lynn—   *"Two years."*

Virginia— *"How long was it that you and the children were a unit by yourselves?"*

Lynn— *"Since Tommy was a year old and Ginny was three. They are now fourteen and sixteen, so I guess that means we were a unit for thirteen years before Jim and I got married."*

Virginia— *"How was that, being the only parent for the children?"* (Personalizing, shifting the focus into the mother.)

Lynn— *"Very difficult."*

Virginia— *"How was it difficult?"*

Lynn— *"I got tired of being the disciplinarian."*

Virginia— *"Had you hoped that Jim would come in and take over that task?"* (Shifting to hopes.)

Jim— (Interjecting.) *"She sure did! She asked me if I would straighten the kids out. They had gotten out of hand."*

Virginia— *"So it was your understanding that Lynn wanted you to take over, Jim?"*

Jim— *"Yes, it was."*

Virginia— *"Lynn, would you agree that you had expressed a wish that Jim take over?"*

Lynn— *"Yes, I guess I did. That seems so long ago."*

Virginia— *"So what was your expectation of what Jim's parenting would be like?"* (Personalizing, shifting to explore for her expectation.)

Lynn— *"Well, I'm not really sure. I just didn't expect him to be so hard on them."*

Virginia— *"You're disappointed that it hasn't turned out the way you had hoped?"* (Reflecting.)

Lynn— *"Yes, I am. But now I see that I wasn't clear about what I wanted."*

Virginia— *"Wonderful. So now let's have you and Jim talk about this and get clear with each other what you expect."* (Reinforcing the lessening of blame and giving guidance.)

Dialogue 2

Sue— *"Jennifer is being very irresponsible! She knows I have to work and it's her job to take care of the younger ones."*

Virginia— *"You are disappointed."* (Shifting to a softer feeling and beginning to personalize by shifting the focus onto the mother's feeling.)

Sue— *"I sure am. It's hard enough to be the only breadwinner since my husband left, but to have to worry about what's going on at home is just too much."*

Virginia— *"You sound like you feel really burdened."* (Reflecting.)

Sue— *"I really do. I need Jennifer to help me. I know it's a lot to ask of a kid, but I need her."*

Virginia— *"I hear you feeling bad for Jennifer, is that right?"* (Bridging.)

Sue— *"Yes, I do. I feel really bad. I wish it wasn't this way."*

Virginia— *"Well, Jennifer, what is going on with you as you hear your mother?"*

Jennifer— *"I feel better, knowing that she can see what it's like for me."*

Differentiating

At the deepest level of change, Satir worked to help people let go of unrealistic expectations, which usually related to earlier internalized expectations of the self or unmet yearnings.

Examples with self:

> *"Are you willing to let go of the impossible expectation of yourself that you should always be there for others?"*
>
> *"As you feel the pain of expecting yourself to be perfect are you willing to let go of that expectation?"*

Examples with mother:

> *"Now that you are an adult and have other resources, are you willing to let go of the expectation that your mother be supportive of you, since she has not been able to do that? Who would be able to be there for you?"*
>
> *"After coming to understand your mother's history of rejection, are you willing to let go of your expectation for her to love you in the way you want to be loved? How do you see yourself getting that need met in your life now?"*

Examples with father:

> *"Knowing that your father is not able to show you approval in the way you want it, are you willing to let go of that expectation? You have other choices now. Where can you look for approval?"*
>
> *"Understanding now that your father did not receive any nurturing from his family, is it possible for you to let go of your expectation for him to nurture you? Who in your current life is capable of nurturing you?"*

PHASE VI— REINFORCING CHANGES

Satir's last phase was that of reinforcing the changes made in the previous phase.

Some of the skills she used to accomplish this were ***reinforcing***, ***anchoring***, and ***using imagery.***

Reinforcing

After guiding someone to make a change, Satir would positively reinforce the change by her words, touch, facial expression, and voice tone.

Examples with individuals:

> *"I'm so glad you were able to get those things out that have been stuck inside."*

> *"Oh, that's wonderful that you could tell me that."*

Examples with couples:

> *"Okay, that's good that you could get that straight with each other."*

> *"How wonderful that you two can now be with each other in this new way."*

Examples with families:

> *"It's marvelous that you could say this to your parents. Now they have new information for understanding you."*

> *"I can see very positive things happening as this family begins to talk with each other in different ways."*

Anchoring

Satir also reinforced changes by underscoring significant changes in perceptions, feelings, beliefs, or behaviors.

Examples with individuals:

> *"How do you feel having shared that with me?"*

> *"Now that you can see the steps toward your goal, how does that feel?"*

Examples with couples:

> *"Be with that new feeling of expressing your feelings to your husband."*

> *"How does it feel to have shared your wants with your wife?"*

Examples with families:

> *"Just be in this new place with your son for a moment."*

> *"Seeing these new possibilities for your family how do you feel at this moment?"*

Using imagery

Often Satir reinforced changes even further by having people imagine themselves maintaining their new ways of being in the future.

Examples with individuals:

> *"Now, Chris, would you be willing to close your eyes and see yourself talking to yourself in this new, kinder way the next time your make a mistake?"*

> *"Can you close your eyes and practice seeing yourself connected with your courage as you begin to take the steps you want to take?"*

Examples with couples:

> *"Having just experienced being straight and clear in your communication with each other here, would you be willing to close your eyes and see yourself doing this at some point in the future?"*

> *"I'm wondering if the two of you would be willing to close your eyes and see yourself being this new way with each other the next time you encounter a difference?"*

Examples with families:

> *"Phyllis, can you just close your eyes and breathe and imagine yourself staying this centered as you talk with your mother-in-law?"*

> *"How about if all of you in this wonderful family just close your eyes for a moment and see yourself in the future being with each other in the new way you have been with each other here today."*

FINAL EXAMPLE

This final example of Satir's work was taken from the videotape "Forgiving Parents," produced by NLP Comprehensive*. This extensive example demonstrates Satir's work in a comprehensive and integrated fashion.

In the example, Satir is working with a woman named Linda who holds resentments toward her mother for being, and having been, extremely critical of her. Linda has asked Satir for help in dealing with her mother's criticism. She describes her mother as criticizing her because she is thin, talks too loud, and doesn't make good use of her musical talent. At the point that the example begins, Satir is asking Linda to consider a different response to her mother's criticism.

Virginia— *"Linda, can you thank your mother for noticing you? Then say to her, 'Mother, I've been meaning to share with you that I know you've often noticed my weight, and I would like to tell you how I feel about my body.'"* (Guiding and modeling.)

"Say the noticing part first, then how you feel about your body. I think your mother worries that you are going to die." (Reframing.)

"You are not thanking her for criticizing you, but for noticing you." (Educating.)

"What does that feel like?" (Exploring feelings.)

Linda— *"I'm confused. When do I say what you are telling me and when do I say that I don't want to hear that I am too skinny anymore?"*

---

*The author thanks Steve Andreas of NLP Comprehensive for permission to use this dialogue taken from the videotape, "Forgiving Parents"

Virginia— *"Well, saying 'thanks for noticing' is the first step. What do you have to do to help yourself to do that?* (Guiding, exploring, specifying.)

Linda— *"It seems like I have to shift my perceptions from seeing my mother's criticism as a way of putting me down to a way of showing me love."*

Virginia— *"Well, it might be loving. I don't know about that for sure, but I think there is some of that. I don't want to push anything down your throat. I can see you still feel rejected and vulnerable."* (Reflecting feelings.)

Linda— *"Yes."*

Virginia— (Asks Linda to choose someone from the group to role-play her mother.) *"Ask your mother if she ever loved and valued you."* (Guiding)

Linda— *"Have you ever loved and valued me?"*

Mother— (Role-player.) *"Yes. I had dreams for you. You were going to be what I couldn't be."*

Virginia— *"Do you believe that, Linda?"* (Exploring beliefs.)

Linda— *"Uh-huh."*

Virginia— *"Come closer, just a step closer to your mother, while you let yourself believe that."* *(Guiding and reinforcing.)*

Virginia— *"What was your mother's life like as a child?"* (Exploring Perception.)

Linda— *"Very hard. Her father was abusive to her."*

Virginia— *"So your mother had a lot of training about how she was bad and not okay?"* (Educating and reframing.)

Linda— *"Yes."*

Virginia— *"I know you know a lot about that too."* (Bridging.)

"Look at your mother, now." (Guiding.)

"What are you feeling?" (Exploring feelings.)

Linda— *"Love and sadness."*

Virginia— *"Just be with that for a moment."* (Anchoring.)

Linda— *"If I were to say everything that I have wanted to say to my mother, both wonderful and painful, it would unleash a lot emotion for her."*

Virginia— *"She would cry. All that happens when people cry is that they get tears. I've never seen any buildings explode!* (Normalizing and challenging implied catastrophic expectation.)

"So, now, look at your mother and talk to her about the things that are wonderful and the things that are painful." (Guiding.)

"Because you know, Linda, this is about you, not your mother. You know that don't you?" (Personalizing.)

Linda— *"Yes."*

Virginia— *"Okay."* (Reinforcing.)

Virginia— *"So as you look at your mother, what is that like for you?"* (Exploring feelings.)

Linda— *"Scary."*

Virginia— *"That's because it's new."* (Educating.)

"Are the odds enough for you to risk doing something you have never done before?" (Challenging.)

Linda— *"I've asked myself that a lot. I feel like I am working on my relationship with my mother already by practicing new ways of interacting with other women."*

Virginia— *"That's not the same. Those women are not your mother."* (Challenging.)

"What are you feeling right now?" (Exploring feelings.)

Linda— *"I'm afraid of coming out of hiding with my mother."*

Virginia— *"I'm hearing your yearning that you want to be loved and valued."* (Identifying the yearning.)

"But a piece of you says, 'Be careful about who you get to love and value you.' Is that true?" (Creating awareness of her defense.)

Linda— *"Uh-huh."*

Virginia— *"So you have your caution in front of you. Could you consider having your caution beside you, instead of in front of you?* (Guiding.)

> *"Can you go inside yourself and know your mother as a human being and know that the way she is had very little to do with you. Do you know that?"* (Educating.)

Linda— *"Yes."*

Virginia— *"But the hurt has gone on for so many years and you are still leaving it all up to your mother."* (Personalizing.)

> *"What about you starting a new process?"* (Challenging.)

> *"Can you recognize that as an adult you have learned new things that you didn't know as a child? Your mother wouldn't know how to do this."* (Educating.)

> *"Could you show her the way?"* (Challenging.)

Linda— *"I'd like to."*

Virginia— *"Look at her now, and let that be what you are in touch with."* (Guiding.)

> *"What does that feel like?"* (Exploring feelings.)

Linda— *"I'm willing. I've been looking for a way."*

Virginia— *"Okay. Now I'd like for you to say, 'Thank you for paying attention to me, and there are some things in the way you pay attention to me that don't fit for me.' "* (Guiding.)

> *"Go up to her and take her hand as you thank her because that is what she needs."* (Educating)

"So that you can say, 'You know, I've been worried about my weight, too. I can't seem to gain.'" (Modeling and guiding.)

"Can you imagine yourself doing that now?" (Using imagery.)

Linda— "Yes."

Virginia— "Let's see what happens as you move it out of your throat." (Guiding.)

Linda— "Mother, thank you for noticing me, but I need to tell you that . . ."

Virginia— "Leave the 'but' off." (Intervening.)

"Let it be a complete sentence by itself." (Guiding.)

Linda— "Mother, I really appreciate you noticing me. The thing with the weight has come up so often. I see that you are worried about me, and I suggest that you not worry because I'm healthy."

Virginia— "Just be in touch with how it feels to be sharing this delicate truthful part of yourself with your mother in a context of acknowledging her presence as well." (Anchoring.)

Linda— "It feels schizophrenic. One part feels good and another part is scared."

Virginia— "Well, the last thing I want is for you to feel you have to do anything different, but if something in you wants to move out in some way or another, then that's okay, too." (Validating.)

Linda— *"I'm feeling fear, trying to let go and transform to love."*

Virginia— *"Give me a picture of your fear."* (Using imagery.)

Linda— *"Opening up communication with my mother so that we say things to each other that would be hurting."*

Virginia— *"Okay, I think I'm getting a sense of this. In your quest to get a new connection with your mother, your fear is, and it might be justified, that you will make things worse. Is that it?"* (Reflecting, validating, and clarifying.)

Linda— *"Yes."*

Virginia— *"Are you aware that you really don't have this to say to your mother, but to your image of your mother?"* (Reframing.)

Linda— *"Intellectually, but I can't seem to bring that through."*

Virginia— *"Here is a pillow that represents your image of your mother. Tell the pillow all of your angers."* (Guiding.)

Linda— *"I want to tell her . . ."*

Virginia— *"Say 'you' to her."* (Intervening and guiding.)

Linda— *"You really hurt me, not being able to ever nurture me, even bathe me."*

Virginia— *"Close your eyes and go inside and see if it's really true that you never got a bath."* (Challenging.)

Linda— *"Well, maybe sometimes . . . but, why couldn't she nurture me. I was a wonderful little baby."*

Virginia— *"Where did you get that idea?"* (Exploring belief.)

Linda— *"I just know I was!"*

Virginia— *"Open your eyes and look at me and see that wonderful part."* (Mirroring and anchoring.)

"Your mother knew that, too." (Educating.)

Linda— *"I know that she did, but she didn't put it out."*

Virginia— *"How long are you going to keep troubling yourself for somebody who had it on the inside but couldn't put it out?"* (Challenging and personalizing.)

Linda— *"I'm looking. I'd like to end it right now."*

Virginia— *"Is there any part of you that doesn't believe she cared about you?"* (Exploring belief.)

Linda— *"Part of her loved me beyond belief and part of her wanted to destroy me."*

Virginia— *"What part loved you?"* (Exploring.)

Linda— *"Her heart."*

Virginia— *"And what part wanted to destroy you?"* (Exploring.)

Linda— *"Her upbringing."*

Virginia— *"This is brilliant. You know what was stopping your mother from expressing what was in her heart."* (Reinforcing.)

Virginia— *"Pick out role-players from the group to come up and be your mother's family. Place them in relation to each other, showing how it was to be in her family."* (Sculpting.)

Linda— (Sculpts her mother's father kicking her mother with the children cowering in front of their abusive father.)

Virginia— *"Shame comes to me so strongly as I look at your mother's family. I can hear your mother saying to you, 'What a shame that you aren't doing more with your music!' "* (Educating as to the origins of the mother's critical behavior.)

Virginia— *"Now this scene gives us a feel for your mother's experience as a child. If we go forward in time, how did your father come on the scene to get together with your mother?"* (Mapping.)

Linda— *"He was funny and he sang. He was attracted to my mother because she was moral, Catholic, and religious."*

Virginia— *"Okay, so he didn't expect her to fool around. Were the women on his side kind of loose?"* (Mapping.)

Linda— *"No. His parents both died when he was very young, and he was raised by his older brother and his brother's wife."*

Virginia— *"Was his brother's wife loose?"*

Linda— *"No."*

Virginia— *"Well, someone was loose in this family, I can tell you that!"* (Educating to systems.)

Linda— *"My father was! He was a wild and crazy kind of guy."*

Virginia— *"Okay, so I want you to think about how people are. Your father is wild and loose and your mother looks like she's full of integrity. Can you imagine that he saw your mother's integrity as a support for him? And she would depend on him to bring light into her life!"* (Educating.)

Virginia— (To Linda's role-play father) *"Go into her mother's family here on stage and rescue her from this family and sing while you do it!"* (Guiding.)

(Role-player father goes into the sculpted mother's family and takes the role-play mother out of the sculpt to a separate part of the stage where they act out singing and having fun together.)

Virginia— *"Now, as you look at your parents, what are you feeling?"* (Exploring feelings.)

Linda— *"They are cute."*

Virginia— *"Just be with that."* (Anchoring new perception.)

Virginia— *"What your father didn't know about your mother is that her rigidity would be over everything, way beyond her integrity."* (Educating.)

"What your mother didn't know about your father is that his funniness would go against her sense of order. So what was used as a way to get together became a yoke around their necks." (Educating and reframing.)

Virginia— *"Let's bring your brothers and sisters up on stage. How many brothers and sisters did you have?"* (Mapping.)

Linda— *"I had one older brother and a younger sister."*

Virginia— *"Okay, choose role-players from the group to be your brother and sister and place them as you experienced them in relation to your parents. Also choose someone to stand in for you in the family."* (Sculpting.)

Linda— *"My brother would be distanced from the family with his back turned and his head bowed."*

Virginia— *"What happened to your brother?"* (Mapping.)

Linda— *"He's an alcoholic."*

Virginia— *"Yes, he would have to do something like that. Being an alcoholic doesn't mean he wasn't bright or nice. It just means when the pain was too great, he drank to numb himself."* (Educating and reframing.)

Virginia— *"What about your sister?"* (Mapping.)

Linda— *"She ran away, became a mother, then ran away from her child, then became a hippie, and now she's a 'born again Christian'."*

Virginia— *"Okay. What did you do?"*

Linda— *"I hung in there and tried to make everybody happy?"*

Virginia— *"Did you succeed even a little bit?"* (Exploring.)

Linda— *"Oh, yeah."*

Virginia— *"Just be with that. How does that feel?"* (Exploring feelings.)

Linda— *"It's a burden."*

Virginia— *"Okay. Now, role-players: I would like for you to take your postures real tight and make sounds and movements that fit your position."* (Making the sculpting come alive.)

"Now, role-players: I'd like for you to give yourself a message of appreciation and take a deep breath, letting your body expand to meet the breath until you are standing on your own two feet and free to move. Now when you get on your own feet, look around and do what you want." (Family role-players end up hugging each other.)

"As you watched, Linda, what did you see happen?" (Exploring her perception.)

Linda— *"Fear transformed into love."*

Virginia— *"Look at your mother; she tried hard but she wasn't all that successful. As you look at her now, what are you aware of feeling?"* (Exploring feelings.)

Linda— *"A lot more compassion."*

Virginia— *"Can you move a little closer and see what that feels like?"* (Guiding and challenging her to change.)

(Linda spontaneously moves all the way over to her mother and hugs her.)

Virginia— *"Be aware that you are now touching the life force of your mother. What you experienced before was the behaviors of your mother because the life force didn't have a place to express itself."* (Anchoring, educating, and reframing.)

(To Linda after she stopped hugging her mother.) *"How was that for you?"* (Anchoring.)

Linda— *"I don't know if I can put it into words. It was very helpful. I have desperately wanted to talk to my mother differently but I was missing the connection for how to do it."*

Virginia— *"Can you see yourself doing it in the future?"* (Using imagery.)

Virginia— *"You have a different expression on your face and in your eyes, which tells me that you have moved to a different place in yourself."* (Anchoring.)

"I don't know what your transactions with your mother will be, but I do know you'll never look at your mother in the same way again. She will never look at you in the same way because you will come in with something different. (Anchoring and educating.)

Linda— *"I feel something has shifted and I think you're right; I won't be able to look at my mother in the same way again. I feel clearer and more loving. Thank you very much for this, Virginia. It was wonderful for me!"*

Three years after the session, a follow-up interview assessing the impact of Satir's work was conducted with Linda by Connie Andreas of NLP Comprehensive. Parts of that interview follow.

Connie—   *"We're interested to find out what has been the impact of your work with Virginia."*

Linda—   *"Well, it was interesting. It has been something that I haven't been able to forget and have talked about with friends. It's affected my relationship with my mother, my work . . . even when I notice the way parents talk to their children, I'm aware of how wonderful the gems were that she had."*

Connie—   *"So it had a fairly broad impact."*

Linda—   *"Oh, I'll never forget it."*

Connie—   *"How has it been different with your mother?"*

Linda—   *"Well, I think that I did a lot of thinking after the session. I came away with a whole lot more compassion about my mother and what she's been through in her life. It's changed my position in how I look at her and how I feel about her."*

Connie—   *"So do you do things differently now than you would have?"*

Linda—   *"Oh, yeah. I look at things differently. I've had lots of occasions to ask her about her life. In fact, she said to me, 'I think my father would have been arrested for child abuse today if he'd done those things to me today.'*

"I've gotten a lot of insights into how she was raised and why she was so critical of me because of some of the things that happened to her. She has opened her heart to me in lots of ways. I feel like her best friend, which is something I would never have said before.

"Having experienced Virginia and watched her work with others, I have incorporated those techniques into my relationship with my mother. I spent lots of time after the session asking my mother questions. If I were taking a day trip somewhere, I would ask her to go along and I would ask her about her life. 'What was your dad like? If you could choose to have kids over again, would you?' I tried to listen very carefully to the answers that she gave. This sounds kind of weird, but I said to myself, 'Boy, Linda, if you think you had it bad having her as a mother, imagine her having them as her parents because she had some tough times. She had immigrant parents who were very hard on her.' "

Connie— *"It sounds like that it has been a lot more positive for you."*

Linda— *"Oh, it has."*

Connie— *"Probably for your mother, too."*

Linda— *"I would think so, but I don't know because she's not the kind of person who shares that stuff. I definitely think, just because she did open up to me, that she feels that way, too. But I had to make the change, you see. For a long time I think I waited for my mother to change. 'Why doesn't she do this or that?' What came out of working with Virginia was that I needed to shift my position or try something else."*

Connie— *"That's a big shift."*

Linda— *"Yeah, it is."*

Connie— *"You mentioned that it's had an impact in some*

other areas, too. Can you say a little more about that?"

Linda— *"My work is as a teacher. I have a consulting business, and I run workshops for parents, community members, and, most recently, youth leadership trainings with high school kids. They will talk to me about their parents because high school kids typically are complaining about their parents, about how they don't listen, pick on them, and never appreciate them for the things they are doing well. I have seen myself doing some of Virginia's tricks where I will say to them, 'You know, you might be the one who needs to talk to your mom first. If you are waiting for your mom to tell you how much she appreciates you, she may not be able to do that. You may have to tell her how much you appreciate what she does for you and that kind of stuff.'"*

Connie— *"So you are passing on your learnings to others, too. Great! Are there any other comments you have about your experience with Virginia?"*

Linda— *"The whole experience of being that open and pouring out that part of me was something I'll never forget. The way that she treated people is a message that I take wherever I go, the respect and dignity that she tried to create between people. In my work of having teens and adults come together to work in partnership, the adults often take over and won't let the teens get a word in edgewise. I use some of the things I learned from Virginia to help them be more on an equal basis."*

Connie— *"Thank you for coming back and letting us know the impact of the session with Virginia for you."*

OVERALL SUMMARY

Satir's work emanated from a philosophy that had five basic tenets. These were

enhancing self-worth is primary;

nurturance is the way to bring about growth;

awareness is the first step toward change;

acceptance of oneself and others is critical to the healing process; and

change is always possible.

The author created an artificial construct outlining the phases of Satir's work and the skills she used within these phases.

PHASE I—MAKING CONTACT

In the first phase of making contact, Satir used the skills of

reaching out,

initiating contact by reaching out with her attitude, her touch, and the proximity of her body;

attending,

taking time to give special attention to each person present;

mirroring,

reflecting through her eyes, facial expression, voice, and touch, her belief in the value of each human being; and

observing,

watching for non-verbal body language cues reflecting feelings.

PHASE II—VALIDATING

In the second phase of validating people and creating a base of trust, she used the skills of

appreciating,

> expressing appreciation for people's efforts and pain;

reassuring,

> expressing a belief in people's desire to do what's best;

affirming,

> acknowledging positive changes and the right to have feelings and wants;

individualizing,

> acknowledging that each person has a right to a point of view and addressing people by name;

engendering hope,

> conveying that change for the better is possible;

reflecting,

> articulating an understanding of a person's position and/or feeling;

clarifying,

> checking out the feeling and/or meaning being conveyed; and

translating,

> offering the underlying message being conveyed.

PHASE III—FACILITATING AWARENESS

In the third phase of working to create awareness, she used the skills of

mapping,

> gathering a detailed family history back through the grandparents;

weaving,

> moving back and forth between the past and the present;

educating,

> giving information about universal principles of human process;

circular questioning,

> asking one person his/her observations of another pair's interaction;

shifting from content to process,

> shifting to the coping process;

identifying dysfunctional process,

> defining the ways in which the person either intrapersonally or interpersonally is not coping in a healthy manner;

sculpting,

> placing people in molded body positions to represent their relationships; and

exploring,

> guiding people to look at themselves, their perceptions, interpretations, feelings, expectations, beliefs, wants, hopes, and yearnings.

PHASE IV—PROMOTING ACCEPTANCE

In the fourth phase of working to gain acceptance of self and others, she used the skills of

normalizing,

> letting people know that what they were feeling was normal and human;

personalizing,

> shifting the focus from the external to the internal;

contracting,

> asking for a willingness to participate;

bridging,

> pointing out similarities; and

reframing,

> shifting the perspective from negative to positive.

PHASE V—MAKING CHANGES

In the fifth phase of making changes, she used the skills of

punctuating,

> stopping dysfunctional process;

modeling,

> demonstrating effective ways of communicating;

guiding,

> giving people directions for how to make changes;

challenging,

> challenging people to make the needed changes;

specifying,

> helping people to speak more specifically;

breaking the rules,

> creating experiences for breaking dysfunctional family rules;

activating dialogues,

> directing people to talk with each other, face to face;

defusing blaming,

> shifting the focus off the person being blamed; and

differentiating,

> assisting people in coming to more realistic expectations.

PHASE VI—REINFORCING CHANGES

In the sixth phase, reinforcing the changes made in the previous phase, she used the skills of

reinforcing,

> positively supporting changes by her words, touch, facial expression, and voice tone;

anchoring,

> underscoring significant changes in perceptions, feelings, beliefs, and behaviors; and

using imagery,

> asking people to imagine themselves continuing their changes in the future.

The skills were identified with a specific phase for the purpose of clarity, but, in reality, many of the skills were used in some or all of the phases.

Appendixes

APPENDIX I.
AID FOR ASSESSING FAMILIES

The acronym **FACADE** has been created to aid therapists in assessing families. Each letter stands for important areas of functioning to assess. The word itself conveys the essence of dysfunctionality, dishonesty.

F   FREEDOM, FUN

How much freedom is present to see and hear what is really happening, to think and feel, to say what you are thinking and feeling, to ask for wants, and to take risks? What are the survival rules and roles which constrict personal freedom? Are any members carrying "the shadows of others" which prevent them from being experienced for themselves? How does the family have fun?

A   ACCEPTANCE, ATTENTION, AFFECTION, and APPRECIATION

Are people accepted and actively appreciated for who they are? Do they feel a sense of belonging? How much time and attention do the parents give to the children? How much affection seems to be present between the members? Do the children get the message that they are lovable, worthwhile and valuable? How supportive are the members of each other? How is sexuality expressed?

C   COMMUNICATION, COMPETENCE, CHOICES and CHANGE

How honest, respectful and caring is the communication? Is information given clearly, openly, directly, and specifically? How is information received? What coping styles are used? Do members speak for themselves or for others? Are the children supported and encouraged in developing skills? Are they supported and encouraged in taking risks? Are they reinforced for their efforts? Are the children given choices? Are they allowed to problem solve age-appropriately? How responsive are the parents to the changing needs of their children? How open are the spouses to learning about themselves and their partner?

A   ANGER

How is anger handled? Directly or indirectly? Respectfully or disrespectfully?

D   DIFFERENCES, DIRECTION, and DEVELOPMENTAL STAGE

Are individual differences celebrated or scorned? Are members valued for their uniqueness? How are differences dealt with? How are decisions made in the family? How are plans carried out? Are the children given direction? Are appropriate limits set for them? Are they protected? Are limits set in such a way as to enhance their dignity? In what developmental stage is the family?

E   ESTEEM, EQUALITY, EXPECTATIONS, and ENMESHMENT

What is the level of each member's self-esteem? How is it expressed? Is self-esteem enhanced or lessened? How is power used between the spouses? How is power used between the parents and the children? What expectations do the spouses have of each other as spouses and as parents? What expectations do they have of their children? Are these appropriate? How clear are the boundaries? Are members given autonomy or do they speak, think, and feel for each other?

APPENDIX II.
FAMILY HISTORY
QUESTIONNAIRE FOR COUPLES

This is a questionnaire designed to help you gain awareness of what you learned from your parents or caretakers that may be affecting your relationship.

How did your parents deal with conflict?

When there was problem in your family, did fault have to be found?

What was the decision-making process in your family?

How did each of your parents deal with anger?

How did each of your parents deal with sadness, grief, loss? Did you lose any pets as a child? If so, how was this loss handled?

How did each of your parents deal with fear? What information did you get about outsiders? Was the world a dangerous place? Were you encouraged or discouraged from taking risks?

Did your family have fun together? If so, how?

How did each of your parents cope with change?

Did your parents show affection towards each other? If so, how?

How were boundaries, such as bedroom, bathroom, and personal privacy, handled in your family?

Who carried the parenting responsibilities? (This can include children.)

How would you describe the self-worth of each of your parents?

When you were a child, was it okay to express your thoughts and feelings?

Was it okay to ask for what you wanted?

What rules were present in your family? (Rules are the messages, often nonverbal, that we pick up about how we are to be.)

What forms of discipline did your parents use?

Was there any abuse? (Abuse includes name-calling, physical hitting, suggestive or demeaning looks, inappropriate touching, intercourse, and rape.)

Were you neglected? (Neglect can include a lack of attention and support as well as the lack of provision for food, shelter, and medical care.)

Were any of the members of your family, including your grandparents, addicted? (Addiction means a pathological relationship to a substance or experience that has life damaging consequences.)

Are you aware of any family secrets? If so, when did you become aware?

APPENDIX III.
COMMON DYSFUNCTIONAL BELIEFS

I have no choices.

I am defective.

I was a mistake.

I am a burden.

I am different from other people.

I am stupid.

I am unlovable.

I am worthless.

I am inadequate.

I don't belong.

I am at fault, always.

It's not okay for me to perceive what is happening.

It's not okay for me to trust my perceptions.

It's not okay to trust others.

It's not okay for me to feel.

It's not okay for me to feel angry.

It's not okay for me to feel scared.

It's not okay for me to say what I think and feel.

It's not okay for me to want.

It's not okay for me to ask for what I want.

It's not okay for me to ask for help.

It's not okay for me to take risks.

It's not okay for me to be different.

Change is to be avoided.

If there is a problem, someone has to be at fault.

There is a right way to do everything.

There are only four directions in life:
good or bad, right or wrong.

Women are impossible to please.

Men / Women can't be trusted.

Men should dominate, women should be subservient.

Feelings dictate behavior.

Sexual feelings are dirty.

Real love means being able to intuit your lover's wants.

All men want is sex.

Sexual rejection means emotional rejection.

The only way to feel okay is to dominate.

Trust means disappointment.

Perception equals reality.

People should do what is expected of them.

Failure equals worthlessness.

Life should be a struggle.

Children are responsible for their parents' pain.

Children see all of their parents.

There is a perfect solution which must be found.

Children are responsible for their sexual behavior with adults.

People who have been sexually abused are damaged goods.

Addictions can be cured with will power.

*It's important to be loyal to family and friends
no matter what they do to you.*

Intelligence proves worth.

One must be competent 100% of the time.

*One must be approved of by those significant to them
100% of the time.*

It's not okay to feel okay.

It's not okay to be relieved.

It's not okay to feel proud.

APPENDIX IV.
COMMONLY HELD YEARNINGS

Some of the yearnings commonly held by people are to be

loved,

lovable,

valued,

esteemed,

wanted,

important,

paid attention to,

accepted,

approved of,

appreciated,

recognized,

touched,

a part of, to belong,

understood.

SOURCES

Carkhuff, Robert, and Anthony, William, *The Skills of Helping* (Amhurst: Human Resource Development Press, Inc., 1979).

Satir, Virginia.
—*Blended Family with a Troubled Boy,* Film (Kansas City, Missouri: Golden Triad Films, 1983).

—*Conjoint Family Therapy, third edition* (Palo Alto: Science and Behavior Books, 1983).

—*Workshop on Family Therapy,* Lectures and Demonstrations (Springfield, Illinois, 1979).

—*Workshop on Working with Couples,* Lectures and Demonstrations (Los Angeles, 1986).

—*Process Community VI,* Lectures and Demonstrations (Crested Butte, Colorado, 1986).

—*Module II,* Lectures and Demonstrations (Crested Butte, Colorado, 1987).

—*Forgiving Parents,* Videotape (Boulder: NLP Comprehensive, 1990).

—*Making Contact* (Millbrae, Celestial Arts, 1976).

—*Promise and Delivery,* Videotape (Chico: Walter Zahnd and Anterra, Inc., 1986).

—*Self-Worth,* Videotape (Boulder: NLP Comprehensive, 1990).

—*The New Peoplemaking* (Palo Alto: Science and Behavior Books, 1988).

—*Your Many Faces* (Millbrae: Celestial Arts, 1975).

Satir, Virginia and Baldwin, Michelle, *Satir Step by Step* (Palo Alto: Science and Behavior Books, 1983).

Schwab, Johanna, *A Resource Handbook For Satir Concepts* (Palo Alto: Science and Behavior Books, 1990).

ABOUT THE AUTHOR

Sharon Loeschen, M.S.W., L.C.S.W., is well recognized as an accomplished psychotherapist and teacher. She received the 1990 "Recognition for Professional Excellence" Award from Family Service of Long Beach, California. She also received the honor of being selected by Virginia Satir to be a member of the Avanta Network, the organization Satir founded as a way of continuing her teachings.

Loeschen received her Master's Degree in Social Work from the University of Illinois in 1966. Since that time she has had a wide range of experiences as a social worker in Illinois, Iowa, and Southern California.

In addition to practicing as a social worker, Loeschen began teaching in 1975 in a systematic counseling skills training program at California State University, Long Beach, under the direction of Dr. Robert Cash. Since then she has taught hundreds of graduate students in effective counseling techniques for individuals, couples and families.

In 1980, Loeschen received her license to practice psychotherapy as a clinical social worker and began an association with Family Service of Long Beach, which she continues to the present.

The Avanta Network, founded in 1977 by Virginia Satir, is an international training organization. Its worldwide members offer training to enhance self-esteem, increase interpersonal communication, and provide a process model for personal and organizational growth. Trainings deepen the participants' understanding of human systems and assist in the process of change.

Avanta-sponsored training events range from week-long to month-long seminars. Members are also available to lead workshops and introduce the Satir model to the public.

For more information, please contact the

Avanta Network
139 Forest Avenue
Palo Alto, California 94301

415-327-1424.